THE GOLDEN YEARS OF RAILR

SOUTHERN PACIFIC IN THE BAY AREA

The San Francisco-Sacramento-Stockton Triangle

GEORGE H. DRURY

KALMBACH BOOKS

Printed in the United States of America

On the cover: Southern Pacific train 52, the *San Joaquin Daylight* to Los Angeles, starts out of Oakland Pier behind 4-8-2 No. 4363. On the next track the *Shasta Daylight* is receiving passengers for points north to Portland. Photo by Richard Steinheimer, February 22, 1950.

Book design: Kristi Ludwig

Copy editor: Mary Algozin

Map: John Signor

Publisher's Cataloging in Publication
Prepared by Quality Books Inc.

Drury, George H.
    Southern Pacific in the Bay Area : the San
Francisco-Sacramento-Stockton triangle / George H. Drury.
    p.   cm. — (Golden years of railroading ; 3)
    Includes bibliographical references and index.
    ISBN 0-89024-274-7

    1. Railroads—California—History—Pictorial works.
    2. Southern Pacific Railway Company—History.   I. Title.

TF20.D78 1996   625.1'009'794
                                 QBI96-40082

CONTENTS

Southern Pacific train 52, the *San Joaquin Daylight* to Los Angeles, starts out of Oakland Pier behind 4-8-2 No. 4363. On the next track the *Shasta Daylight* is receiving passengers for points north to Portland. Photo by Richard Steinheimer, February 22, 1950.

SOUTHERN PACIFIC

Until the merger era that began with the creation of the Burlington Northern, Southern Pacific was one of the largest railroads in the United States. It ranked third behind the Pennsylvania and the New York Central in operating revenue, and it was second only to the Santa Fe in route mileage. SP's lines stretched over a greater distance than any other American railroad: from Portland, Oregon, south to Los Angeles, then east to New Orleans, from San Francisco east to Ogden, Utah, and, until 1951, from Tucson, Arizona, down the west coast of Mexico to Guadalajara. It dominated transportation in California, and it was the only large railroad headquartered on the West Coast.

It is easiest to explain Southern Pacific's history route by route, much as its passenger timetables were arranged years ago.

Overland Route (Central Pacific)

The Sacramento Valley Rail Road opened in 1856 from Sacramento east to Folsom and Placerville. Its line was laid out by Theodore D. Judah, who intended to continue the line beyond Placerville over the Sierra Nevada to Virginia City, Nevada. He sought financial backing in San Francisco and was rebuffed — that city considered itself a seaport, not the terminus of a railroad. Judah found more interest in Sacramento, also a port and the commercial center of the California gold rush. The Central Pacific Rail Road of California was incorporated on June 28, 1861, by four Sacramento merchants: Leland Stanford, Collis P. Huntington, Mark Hopkins, and Charles Crocker — the Big Four.

California was admitted to the union in 1850. It needed a railroad to connect it to the rest of the country, but the route of that railroad posed a question: south toward the slave states or north toward the free states. The secession of the slave states settled the question. In 1862 Congress passed the Pacific Railroad Act, which provided for the incorporation of the Union Pacific Railroad to build westward and empowered the Central Pacific to build east to meet the Union Pacific. The Act also provided loans and land for both railroads.

A parenthetical note on the land grants: The federal government gave the railroads alternate square miles of land along the route. The land was of little value without the railroad; with the railroad in place the government could get a higher price for the remaining land. The land grants also included provisions for reduced-rate transportation for mail, government property, and employees. By the time those provisions were repealed in 1946 the government had received more than ten times the value of the land in transportation.

Construction of the Central Pacific began at Sacramento in January 1863. By 1867 the rails had crossed the state line into Nevada. On May 10, 1869, the rails of the Central Pacific and the Union Pacific were joined at Promontory, Utah, completing the first railroad across North America — a gold spike and a laurel tie marked the occasion.

Soon afterward the Central Pacific purchased Union Pacific's track from Promontory southeast to Ogden, which was already an established city and better suited to be a junction between the two railroads than Promontory.

The four men who controlled the Central Pacific also controlled the Southern Pacific, and the two roads were operated as a unified system. By 1884 it was clear that corporate simplification was necessary. The most logical proposal, consolidating the two companies, was rejected. A new Southern Pacific Company was formed to replace the Southern Pacific Railroad. The Central Pacific Railroad leased its properties to the SP and was reorganized as the Central Pacific Railway.

As the 19th century closed, control of SP rested with C. P. Huntington, last survivor of the Big Four. Huntington died in 1900, and his SP stock was purchased by the Union Pacific, which had recently come under the control of E. H. Harriman. Harriman acquired a UP that had fallen on hard times. It consisted essentially of lines from Omaha and Kansas City west through Cheyenne to Ogden. Harriman immediately undertook a complete rebuilding of the UP and reacquired the route northwest through Idaho to Portland, Oregon, that had been lost a few years before. Without ownership or control of the Central Pacific from Ogden to California, though, UP's line to Ogden was worthless.

The Southern Pacific was in good condition, but Harriman soon undertook two major improvements on the Overland Route: the Lucin Cutoff across the Great Salt Lake, shortening the Oakland-Ogden distance by 44 miles (and bypassing Promontory), and a second track over the Sierra, in many places with an easier grade — plus automatic block signaling.

Meanwhile President Theodore Roosevelt had begun to consider the problems that big business posed for the free enterprise system, and he focused his attention on Harriman, the Union Pacific, and the Southern Pacific (and matters weren't helped by Frank Norris's muckraking novel, *The*

Octopus). The upshot was that UP had to sell its SP stock and SP had to justify its retention of Central Pacific — and the latter process went on for years, consuming management time and creating an atmosphere of uncertainty.

Divestiture of Central Pacific would have ripped the heart out of SP's network of lines in California and Oregon. Central Pacific's principal routes were from Oakland and San Jose over Altamont Pass to Sacramento, then to Ogden, from Fernley, Nevada, northwest to Susanville, Calif.; from Roseville north to Hornbrook, Calif., on the Siskiyou Route and to Kirk, Oregon, north of Klamath Falls; and from Stockton through Fresno to Goshen Junction (the Natron Cutoff and the Modoc line, both built in the late 1920s, were also Central Pacific routes.) Central Pacific's corporate existence continued until 1959.

Central and Southern California

The San Francisco & San Jose Railroad opened between the cities of its title in 1864, and in 1865 its owners incorporated the Southern Pacific Railroad to build south and east to New Orleans. History is unclear as to the next few years — who acquired whom, what was incorporated when — but by 1870 the Southern Pacific (possibly a new Southern Pacific) and the San Francisco & San Jose were in the hands of the Big Four. Construction started southeast from San Jose, and by 1871 the line had reached Tres Pinos, in the mountains east of Salinas and west — a long way west — of Fresno. There was almost no population to support a railroad beyond Tres Pinos, so Southern Pacific changed its plans and started construction southeast through the San Joaquin Valley from Lathrop, 9 miles south of Stockton. The rails reached Fresno in 1872 and Sumner, across the Kern River from Bakersfield, at the end of 1874. The line was built by the Central Pacific as far south as Goshen Junction, 53 miles south of Fresno, where it intersected the original Southern Pacific survey. Beyond Goshen Junction it was built by Southern Pacific.

The Tehachapi Mountains form the south end of the valley. To keep the grade over the mountains within limits, William Hood laid out a tortuous line that twists back and forth and at one point crosses over itself. The line reached a summit at Tehachapi, then descended directly to the northwest corner of the Mojave Desert. SP had intended to build southeast across the Mojave Desert to the Colorado River but it was induced to detour through Los Angeles, then barely more than a mission.

SP also built east across the Mojave Desert, meeting the Santa Fe at Needles, California, in 1883. It later traded the Mojave-Needles line to the Santa Fe for the Sonora Railway, which ran from Nogales, Arizona, south to the Gulf of California at Guaymas. The Sonora Railway became the Southern Pacific of Mexico and later the Ferrocarril del Pacifico.

The line along the coast between San Francisco and Los Angeles was completed in 1901. In 1967 SP opened the Palmdale-Colton Cutoff along the north edge of the San Gabriel Mountains and over Cajon Pass. The line allows through freight trains to bypass Los Angeles.

Sunset and Golden State Routes

From Los Angeles the Southern Pacific built east through Colton and over San Gorgonio Pass, reaching the Colorado River at Yuma, Arizona, in 1877. Further construction, as the Galveston, Harrisburg & San Antonio Railway, put the line across the Rio Grande into El Paso, Texas, in 1881. In 1883 on the bank of the Pecos River it met a line being built west from San Antonio.

In 1924 SP acquired the El Paso & Southwestern system, which reached from Tucson through Douglas, Ariz., and El Paso to Tucumcari, New Mexico, where it connected with the Rock Island. The El Paso-Tucumcari line was opened in 1902; the Rock Island line from Tucumcari through Kansas City to St. Louis was acquired by SP subsidiary Cotton Belt in 1980.

Texas and Louisiana Lines

Texans are quick to point out that SP's earliest ancestors were the Buffalo Bayou, Brazos & Colorado and New Orleans, Opelousas & Great Western railroads, both chartered in 1850. The BBB&C was reorganized in 1870 as the Galveston, Harrisburg & San Antonio Railway. Its line reached San Antonio in 1877, engaged in some machinations with and against Jay Gould's Missouri Pacific system, and continued building westward. The Opelousas, sold in 1869 to steamship magnate Charles Morgan and later resold and reorganized as Morgan's Louisiana & Texas Railroad, built across the bayou country west of New Orleans to form a New Orleans-Houston route in conjunction with the Louisiana Western and the Texas & New Orleans.

In 1934 all these railroads were consolidated as the Texas & New Orleans Railroad. Even after the repeal in 1967 of the article in the Texas constitution requiring railroads operating in Texas to be headquartered there, the T&NO lines were operated separately.

Shasta and Cascade Routes

In 1870 the Central Pacific acquired the California & Oregon Railroad, which had built northward from Marysville, California. Construction continued north through the Sacramento Canyon and over the Siskiyou Range to connect with the Oregon & California Railroad at Ashland, Oregon, in 1887, putting SP in Portland (the O&C became part of the SP system when the routes were joined). Because the line over the Siskiyous was steep and tortuous, in 1926 SP opened the Natron Cutoff between Klamath Falls and Eugene, Ore. (it had earlier built northeast to Klamath Falls), creating a much easier route that was about 25 miles shorter. About the same time SP opened a line from Klamath Falls southeast to the Overland Route at Fernley, Nevada, to create a shortcut for freight — largely lumber — moving east from Oregon. Part of the Modoc Line was new construction; other portions used the right of way of the 3-foot-gauge Nevada-California-Oregon Railway.

Subsidiaries

SP's largest electric subsidiary was the Pacific Electric Railway, which was assembled by Henry E. Huntington, nephew and heir of Collis P. Huntington. It was the largest electric railway in the country. It was centered on Los Angeles and reached from Santa Monica on the coast inland past San Bernardino, and from San Fernando south to Balboa.

In 1907 SP and Santa Fe formed the jointly owned Northwestern Pacific Railroad, which consolidated several short railroads north of San Francisco. In 1914 it completed its line north through the redwood country and down the Eel River canyon to Eureka. SP bought out Santa Fe's share in 1929. It sold the north end of the line in 1984 and has recently leased the south half to the California Northern Railroad.

The St. Louis Southwestern Railway (the Cotton Belt) is SP's principal subsidiary. It grew from a 3-foot gauge predecessor that began life as a feeder to the Texas & Pacific. It built an extension north to the Mississippi River opposite Cairo, Illinois, and became part of a narrow gauge system reaching from Toledo, Ohio, to Mexico City. Then it converted to standard gauge, expanded throughout northeast Texas, negotiated trackage rights to Memphis and St. Louis, and settled down to an existence as a bridge route between Texas and St. Louis. In the 1920s first the Rock Island, then the Kansas City Southern considered acquiring the Cotton Belt. KCS lost interest in it about the time Southern Pacific was seeking a connection to St. Louis from its Texas lines. SP control began in 1932, and for the past several decades the Cotton Belt has been essentially a division of SP.

Southern Pacific acquired the Sonora Railway from the Santa Fe in exchange for the Mojave-Needles line. In retrospect it appears Santa Fe got the better deal — a strategic section of its main line. SP anticipated good volumes of freight and passenger traffic as the west coast of Mexico developed. It incorporated the Southern Pacific Railroad of Mexico in 1909 to extend the Sonora Railway southward to a connection with the National Railways of Mexico near Guadalajara. Construction of the line was hampered by wild, rough country, Indian uprisings, and the Mexican revolution. The line was not completed until 1927, and for several years thereafter further revolutionary activity interrupted service.

The 1,095-mile line from the border at Nogales to Guadalajara was expensive to build and operate and brought in little revenue. In December 1951 SP sold the Southern Pacific of Mexico to the Mexican government. It was renamed the Ferrocarril del Pacifico (Pacific Railroad). It gradually redeemed itself and developed a good business moving fresh fruit and vegetables northward. It became part of the National Railways of Mexico in 1987.

Southern Pacific fell on hard times in the 1970s — not the begging-on-street-corners poverty of the Rock Island and the Milwaukee Road but at least significant belt-tightening. The expanding

Union Pacific swallowed the Western Pacific and diverted considerable traffic from SP's line over Donner Pass to the former WP line through Feather River Canyon.

SP and Santa Fe announced merger plans in 1980, then called it off, then tried again in 1983. Santa Fe Industries and Southern Pacific Company, the parent companies of the two railroads, were merged by Santa Fe Southern Pacific Corporation on December 23, 1983. The two railroads continued to operate separately, but they began to repaint locomotives and letter them either SP__ or __SF, so they could easily become SPSF when the Interstate Commerce Commission approved the formation of the Southern Pacific & Santa Fe Railway — which on July 24, 1986, it didn't.

Santa Fe Southern Pacific appealed, making peace with the major protesters (Union Pacific and Denver & Rio Grande Western). The ICC did not change its mind and required SFSP to divest itself of a railroad. On October 13, 1988, SP was purchased by Rio Grande Industries, parent company of the Denver & Rio Grande Western Railroad. The railroad resulting from this purchase has dark gray, red-nosed diesels lettered "Southern Pacific" and is headquartered in Denver.

The merger of Burlington Northern and Santa Fe in 1995 changed the western railroad situation again: BNSF's map looks like a dragon about to chomp down on SP. On August 3, 1995, Union Pacific and Southern Pacific announced their intention to merge. The merger was approved by the Surface Transportation Board (successor to the ICC) on July 3, 1996.

Recommended reading: *The Southern Pacific, 1901-1985,* by Don L. Hofsommer, published in 1986 by Texas A&M University Press, College Station, TX 77843-4354 (ISBN 0-89096-246-4)

Now for a few clarifications and definitions. All across the Southern Pacific system trains were labeled westward if they were headed toward San Francisco and eastward if they were headed away from San Francisco — whether toward Los Angeles, Ogden, or Portland, regardless of compass direction. Westward trains carried odd numbers; eastward, even. The only exception in the Bay Area was between Lathrop (south of Stockton) and Polk (east of Sacramento), where westward was defined as from Tracy to Polk (north by the compass), and westward trains carried odd numbers. It's worth noting that geographically Portland is 12 minutes of longitude west of San Francisco, and Los Angeles is about as far east of San Francisco as it is south.

A few locally used geographical terms are worth noting. The East Bay is the area along the east shore of San Francisco Bay. The Peninsula is the area between San Francisco and San Jose. "Down the Peninsula" means toward San Jose, up is toward San Francisco. San Francisco is The City. Don't call it Frisco.

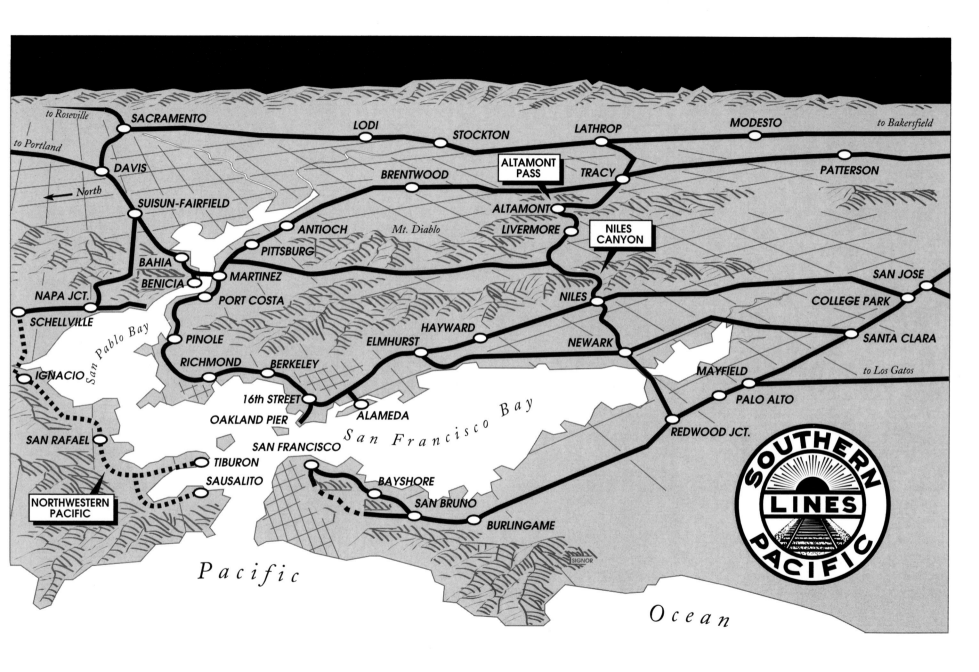

Long-distance trains were a minority at Third Street Station. Most of the trains looked like train 118, a midday local to San Jose. Photo by Don Howe.

San Francisco to San Jose

San Francisco, already well established as a city and a seaport, had little interest in the Central Pacific, but it had railroads of its own. The San Francisco & San Jose Railroad was incorporated on August 18, 1860, and completed a line between the cities of its name on June 6, 1864.

The San Francisco & San Jose was involved early with two transcontinental schemes. It was intended to be the San Francisco connection of the original Western Pacific, but the routes up the east side of the bay to Oakland were much more direct — and the route over Altamont Pass was superseded by the direct route through Benicia and Port Costa. It was also the first link in the original Southern Pacific proposal, the one that got as far as Tres Pinos before its backers changed their minds and made a fresh start down the San Joaquin Valley.

Even if it missed its transcontinental destinies, the line along the Peninsula was a busy part of the Southern Pacific. It was the only all-rail freight route to San Francisco, and it was the north end of SP's Coast Route, shorter and more scenic than the route through the San Joaquin Valley. And it did carry a transcontinental train, if you count the Gulf of Mexico as part of the Atlantic: the *Sunset Limited* operated between New Orleans and San Francisco via the Coast Line from December 1901 to January 1942, with a brief hiatus in 1935 and 1936.

Southern Pacific had two principal passenger stations in San Francisco. The route up the Peninsula from San Jose terminated at a mission-style station at Third and Townsend streets. The building was intended to be temporary — a new station on the ground floor of SP's general office building at 65 Market Street, opposite the Ferry Building, was to take its place after the 1915 Panama-Pacific Exposition. Plans for the extension and the new station were dropped about the time Union Pacific control of SP ended in 1913.

Third Street Station was almost a mile from Market Street, San Francisco's principal thoroughfare. Several streetcar and bus routes connected the station with the business district of the city, and many commuters walked to and from their trains. In the years after 1913 there were numerous proposals for a station nearer the business district, but all that came of them was the 1976 razing of Third Street Station. It was replaced by a small structure at Fourth and Townsend, a block farther from the city's business district.

For years Southern Pacific operated the only steam-railroad commuter service in the West ("West" meaning the territory west of Missouri Pacific's St. Louis-Pacific, Mo., train). It was not simply one or two trains to San Francisco in the morning and out at night; it was an all-day-and-evening, both-directions suburban service. A minor SP peculiarity made it "commute" service, not "commuter." The schedules allowed reverse commuting (to the suburbs in the morning, back to the city in the evening) and let city dwellers spend an evening with friends in the suburbs (and vice versa).

The highlight of SP's commute operation was the evening rush hour, when five trains departed from Third Street at 3-minute intervals between 5:14 and 5:26 and ran nonstop down the Peninsula until about 5:55, when all the trains made their first stop, then continued south making all or most station stops. Thus most Peninsula commuters got home a little after 6 p.m. Morning trains had a somewhat more complicated schedule that offered a choice of departure times and a fast ride from most stations. Peninsula commuters for the most part rode in coaches that were not castoffs from mainline passenger service. Many of the trains were equipped with what SP called "interurban" coaches, 96-passenger cars built in 1924 and 1927. In 1955 the first of three batches of air-conditioned gallery cars arrived to replace the few downgraded mainline coaches.

No passenger trains entered Southern Pacific's other passenger station, the Ferry Building at the foot of Market Street. There passengers boarded ferries for the 20-minute trip to Oakland Pier. Most of the ferry passengers were commuters until the electric suburban trains were shifted to the Bay Bridge on January 15, 1939. The ferries continued to carry long-distance passengers to and from Oakland Pier until July 29, 1958. They were replaced by buses operating to and from the Ferry Building, but by mid-1959 SP had consolidated its San Francisco passenger facilities at Third Street.

There was briefly a third SP terminal in San Francisco. From January 1939 to July 1941 the electric suburban trains of SP's Interurban Electric Railway operated over the San Francisco-Oakland Bay Bridge into the Eastbay Terminal at First and Mission streets.

The premier freight train on the Peninsula was the *Overnight*, which carried less-than-carload merchandise overnight between San Francisco and Los Angeles (and intermediate points) at passenger-train speeds. Specially painted boxcars were assigned to the trains; *Daylight* 4-8-4s were the customary motive power. The *Overnights* were the subject of an article in the August 1950 issue of *Railroad Magazine*, and two items from that article are noteworthy. The average load per boxcar was 18,000 pounds (9 tons), and in the consist of the train the reporter had ridden was a flat car with a truck trailer body on it. The reporter predicted that within a year SP would be moving entire trains of truck trailers on flat cars.

Third Street Station, San Francisco. SP photo.

Two passengers have already staked out the rear seats in the parlor-observation car of the *Morning Daylight* as it awaits departure from Third Street Station about 1950. SP photo.

At the outer end of the platform, the white plume above the pop valves of GS-4 No. 4453 indicates that steam is up and departure of the *Morning Daylight* is imminent. Photo by R. D. McIntyre, 1952.

Train 118, an early-afternoon train, has a *Daylight* car tucked behind the tender of its Pacific in this view north of Tunnel 5. Photo by Reginald McGovern, April 1951.

Pacific 2436, built by Baldwin in 1911 and rebuilt in 1928, hustles train 133 toward San Francisco near Lomita, a station between San Bruno and Millbrae closed in 1962. The first two cars are lounge cars, pressed into emergency use as coaches during World War II. Photo by Otto J. Brechtelsbauer.

Pacific 2472 has a string of older coaches in tow in this early-1940s view. SP photo.

Emerging briefly from the shade of a row of eucalyptus trees, train 138, with 4-8-2 No. 4312 in charge, speeds past train 99, the northbound *Daylight,* at Oak Grove Avenue in Burlingame. The commute left Third Street Station at 5:26 and will make its first stop at Belmont, 22 miles out, at 5:53; the *Daylight* left Los Angeles at 8:15 and will be in San Francisco at 6 p.m. Photo by Fred Matthews, June 1954.

Pacific 2424, a member of SP's first group of Pacifics, starts a three-car train out of San Mateo. Photo by Don Howe.

The *Noon Daylight* has barely begun its 10-hour trip to Los Angeles as it swings through a gentle curve at Belmont. In place of the customary streamlined 4-8-4 is a two-unit set of *Golden State* E7s. Photo by Henry Hughes.

Train Master 4802 rolls into San Jose at the head of train 126, a late-afternoon local from San Francisco. Photo by Kenneth L. Douglas, June 14, 1957.

Under the same signal bridge rolls train 143 starting its noontime trip to San Francisco behind No. 2476. Photo by Don Howe.

It is obvious that Mountain type 4305 isn't stopping at Menlo Park. On its drawbar are 16 cars of football fans eager for the Big Game (University of California vs. Stanford) at the Stanford Stadium. Photo by Fred Matthews, November 1953.

It's the day of the Big Game (Cal-Stanford), and SP has used so many of its commute coaches for special trains that it has had to borrow five streamlined coaches (two articulated pairs and a single) for local service from the *Starlight* during its daytime layover. Passengers were hesitant to board, thinking the train was the second section of the *Daylight*. Photos by Fred Matthews, November 24, 1951.

DAYLIGHT 4-8-4

In 1937 Southern Pacific streamlined its Los Angeles-San Francisco daytime express, the *Daylight*, with 24 cars from Pullman and six 4-8-4s from Lima Locomotive Works. The cars were painted red, orange, and black and lettered and lined in aluminum — "stunning" understates the effect the color scheme must have had on a public accustomed to SP's usual dark-olive passenger cars. The 4-8-4s were painted to match and actually carried a minimal amount of sheet-metal streamlining: running-board skirts, a "skyline" casing along the top of the boiler, and a conical smokebox door. They were among the best-looking streamlined steam locomotives.

The first *Daylight* 4-8-4s, the GS-2 class, were SP's second 4-8-4s. SP's first 4-8-4s had come from Baldwin in 1930: Nos. 4400-4409 for Pacific Lines (SPs lines west of El Paso, Texas) and 700-703 for the Texas & Louisiana Lines (lines east of El Paso). They were classed GS-1 — some say for "General Service" and others say for "Golden State." They were modest-size Northerns weighing 442,300 pounds; they had 73-inch drivers and 27-by-30-inch cylinders. (The renumbering of the GS-1s as they were transferred back and forth between Pacific Lines and T&L Lines is too muddled to recount here.)

The six *Daylight* 4-8-4s, Nos. 4410-4415, were built by Lima in late 1936, as were all subsequent SP 4-8-4s. Dimensionally they were the same as the GS-1s, but they were streamlined. In 1937 Lima delivered another 14 with 80-inch drivers, 26-by-32-inch cylinders, and 280 pounds boiler pressure: GS-3s 4416-4429. They were followed by the 28 GS-4s and two GS-5s in 1941 and 1942: half an inch less cylinder diameter and 20 pounds higher pressure. The two GS-5s were identical to the GS-4s except for roller bearings, Timken on No. 4458 and SKF on 4459. The 4-8-4s went to work on all the principal passenger trains and also the San Francisco-Los Angeles *Overnight* merchandise freight trains.

The GS-6 locomotives were built under wartime restrictions. They were required to be dual-service engines, not passenger power, so they reverted to the 73-inch-driver GS-2 design; they lacked skirting and were painted black. (Western Pacific received six identical engines, and Central of Georgia used the same design for its "Big Apple" 4-8-4s.)

GS-4 No. 4449 was placed on display in Portland, Oregon, in 1958. It was restored to operating condition in 1975 for the American Freedom Train, then regained its *Daylight* colors and has since operated over much of the SP system.

In 1952 SP leased 11 Cotton Belt 4-8-4s that had been displaced by diesels, classified them GS-7 and GS-8, and got another three to five years' service out of them, first on on the Rio Grande Division out of El Paso, then in San Francisco commute service.

Recommended reading: *Those Daylight 4-8-4s,* by Robert J. Church, published in 1996 by Kratville Publications, 2566 Farnam Street, Omaha, NE 68131.

Type	Class	Numbers	Qty	Builder	Built	Retired	Notes
4-8-4	GS-1	4400-4409	10	Baldwin	1930	1954-1957	
4-8-4	GS-1	700-703	4	Baldwin	1930	1954-1956	Texas & Louisiana Lines
4-8-4	GS-2	4410-4415	6	Lima	1936	1954-1958	
4-8-4	GS-3	4416-4429	14	Lima	1937	1954-1958	
4-8-4	GS-4	4430-4457	28	Lima	1941-1942	1956-1958	
4-8-4	GS-5	4458, 4459	2	Lima	1942	1958, 1956	Roller bearings
4-8-4	GS-6	4460-4469	10	Lima	1943	1954-1958	
4-8-4	GS-7	4475-4481	7	Baldwin	1930	1955-1957	Ex-Cotton Belt
4-8-4	GS-8	4485-4488	4	StLSW	1937, 1942	1956, 1958	Ex-Cotton Belt

When the *Daylight* was introduced, SP advertised it as "The most beautiful train in the world." Little can be said to support any opposing viewpoint as train 98, the *Coast Daylight,* starts south out of San Jose after a pause to add two coaches from Oakland to its consist. Next stop: Salinas, 68 miles away. Photo by Richard Steinheimer, March 1954.

THE LOS GATOS BRANCH

SP's Peninsula lines included a second branch in addition to the old line between San Francisco and San Bruno via Daly City. It diverged south at Mayfield (later renamed California Avenue) south of Palo Alto and ran more or less southeasterly through Los Altos, Cupertino, and Saratoga to Vasona Junction, then turned south to Los Gatos. The Mayfield-Vasona Junction portion of the line was at one time shared with the Peninsular Railway, an electric subsidiary of the SP (it ceased operation in 1933); the Vasona Junction-Los Gatos segment was part of the former South Pacific Coast Railroad from Alameda through San Jose to Santa Cruz. Until 1940 the line carried San Francisco-Santa Cruz trains.

In later years the Los Gatos branch was an interesting operation. Between San Francisco and Los Gatos the train operated conventionally, but the equipment was stored overnight at San Jose. Because there were no engine-turning facilities at Los Gatos, the engine ran around the train there and then ran backwards, pulling the empty train to San Jose. The process was reversed in the morning. The last train to Los Gatos ran January 3, 1964, and much of the route of the Mayfield-Vasona Junction branch has been used for highways.

Pacific type 2476, built by Lima in 1917 for the Arizona Eastern, brakes for the stop at Los Altos station with train 166, a Saturday-only local from San Francisco. Until the mid-1950s and the end of the 5½-day work week, early-afternoon Saturday trains were common in most commuter operations. Later that afternoon 2476 brings the empty equipment from Los Gatos to San Jose as train 191. Photos by Fred Matthews, September 29, 1951.

Like 2476, Pacific 2410 was fitted with a pilot on the rear of its tender for the 9-mile trip in reverse between Los Gatos and San Jose. Photo by Richard Houghton, 1947.

Alco PA-2 No. 6028 rests in the sun at the west end of the Oakland Pier trainshed after bringing train 27, the *Overland,* from Ogden, Utah, and points east. In the adjacent slip *San Leandro* loads passengers for the trip across the bay. The careers of SP's ferries and Oakland Pier have little more than six weeks to go. Photo by John C. Illman, June 15, 1958.

OAKLAND PIER

San Franciscans and Oaklanders agree that Oakland is not San Francisco, but Southern Pacific's principal San Francisco station for long-distance passenger trains was in Oakland: Oakland Pier (often called Oakland Mole). Equipment listings in passenger timetables said "San Francisco," not "Oakland," but there was no way you could occupy your roomette from Portland all the way to San Francisco. You had to get off the train at Oakland Pier and onto a ferry for the last 3½ miles. Oakland Pier was closer to San Francisco than it was to downtown Oakland — and a lot closer to San Francisco than is today's San Francisco International Airport. (Oakland had its own mainline stations at 16th Street on the line to Martinez and on First Street at Jack London Square on the line to San Jose.)

SP had two ancestors on the east shore of the bay, each with its own terminal. The San Francisco & Oakland used the predecessor of Oakland Pier, and the San Francisco & Alameda had a similar terminal on a long pier at Alameda. Between the two was San Antonio Creek. Years later the Western Pacific (Gould's Western Pacific) built its terminal directly across San Antonio Creek from the Alameda pier. The Santa Fe, like the WP a latecomer to the Bay Area, had a ferry slip at Ferry Point in Richmond. It later acquired a line down through Berkeley to Oakland, running in streets much of the way.

In 1933 Western Pacific and Santa Fe both moved their passenger operations to SP's Oakland Pier station. In 1939 the Santa Fe built a new station at 40th Street and San Pablo Avenue, handy to the east end of the Bay Bridge, and about the same time opened a bus station on Fourth Street in San Francisco. It moved its passengers from SP's ferries to a new bus service over the Bay Bridge. Santa Fe pulled back to a terminal at Richmond in 1958. WP remained at Oakland Pier until it closed in 1958, then substituted a bus between an unsheltered platform at Middle Harbor Road in the Oakland yards and Santa Fe's bus terminal on Fourth Street in San Francisco.

Economics finally caught up with Oakland Pier and the ferries. The cost of chartering a few buses to operate between 16th Street Station in Oakland and Third Street Station in San Francisco was far less than the cost of maintaining even a minimal fleet of ferries (and both boats were old and in need of overhaul) and the Oakland Pier station and the passenger facilities in the Ferry Building in San Francisco. SP's ferries ran for the last time on July 29, 1958. Oakland Pier continued to serve as the terminal for a brief period until bus transfer facilities were added to 16th Street Station. Within a few months SP closed its Ferry Building facilities and consolidated its San Francisco station operations at Third Street.

Recommended reading: *Southern Pacific Bay Area Steam*, by Harre W. Demoro, published in 1979 by Chatham Publishing Company, P. O. Box 283, Burlingame, CA 94010. (ISBN 0-89685-037-4)

Ferry steamer *Eureka* starts east across the bay with passengers for train 10, the *Shasta Daylight,* which will leave Oakland Pier for Portland at 8:15 a.m. The boat is a former Northwestern Pacific ferry; it came to SP when NWP gave up commuter service in 1941. Photo by Fred Matthews, April 15, 1951.

Deckhands prepare for mooring as a ferry approaches Oakland Pier. Main deck passengers and baggage carts will go straight ahead into the main shed; passengers can also unload to the left and right from the upper deck. Photo by Richard Steinheimer, April 29, 1950.

The *Shasta Daylight* stands on track 9 ready to receive passengers half an hour before departure. It is coupled to station air and steam lines so the dining car crew may prepare breakfast — steam for coffee urns and steam tables and air to pressurize the water system. The trainsets built in 1949 for the *Shasta* did not include parlor-observation cars; SP chose to reassign cars that had been built in 1941 for the *Morning Daylight.* Photo by Richard Steinheimer, February 22, 1950.

(Opposite) Alco's PA-1 passenger diesel, SP's scarlet-and-orange *Daylight* livery, and the Budd-built *California Zephyr* were esthetic high points of the streamliner era. The fortunate could enjoy all three at once at Oakland Pier, where SP 6006 stands at the head of the *Cascade,* just in from Portland. Across the platform is the *California Zephyr,* waiting for its passengers to arrive from San Francisco by ferry. Two SP men discuss the mechanics of the PA-1 while Western Pacific's train crew and the Zephyrette hostess plus a Shore Patrol officer stand by. Photo by Richard Steinheimer.

TRA 9

NO. 10

Shasta Daylight
DEPARTS
8:15 A.M. DAILY

MARTINEZ
DAVIS
GERBER
REDDING
DUNSMUIR
KLAMATH FALLS
EUGENE
ALBANY
SALEM
PORTLAND

Beyond the end of the trainshed train 52, the *San Joaquin Daylight,* starts out for Los Angeles behind 4-8-2 No. 4363. Visible across the platform are the three Alco PAs and the mail-baggage car of the *Shasta Daylight.* Photo by Richard Steinheimer, February 22, 1950.

Train 224, the *Senator* for Sacramento, accelerates out of Oakland Pier behind GP9 No. 5622 while GS-4 No. 4448 simmers at the head of the *San Joaquin Daylight.* When 52's departure time comes, the 4-8-4 leaves no doubt that it is departing. The train includes a heavyweight dining car and one of SP's homebuilt domes. Both photos by Robert Hale.

Train 56, the San Joaquin Valley local (once the *Tehachapi*), departs Oakland Pier on its last run behind Pacific 2475. Its leisurely trip to Los Angeles will take 20 hours. Photo by John C. Illman, January 8, 1955.

The consist of train 27, the *San Francisco Overland,* moves toward the West Oakland coach yard behind 0-6-0 No. 1293, a Lima product of 1924. The parlor-observation car on the rear operated only between Reno and Oakland. Photo by Fred Matthews, February 3, 1952.

Late afternoon was a busy time at Oakland Pier. Western Pacific's *California Zephyr* arrived at 4:15, SP train 102, the *City of San Francisco,* left at 5:27, and the *Cascade* left for Portland at 5:32. The *City* is shown here with three Alcos; visible beyond it are two coaches of the *Cascade.* Photo by Fred Matthews, February 3, 1952.

Alco diesels lead the *San Francisco Overland,* train 27, into the trainshed. Photo by John C. Illman, June 15, 1958.

The *City of San Francisco* became a daily train on September 1, 1947. The sign at the end of track 9 predates daily operation, and the wording, "The Streamliner *City of San Francisco* Sails To-day," is a reminder of the era when Union Pacific's streamliners didn't simply depart but sailed. The humbler, unstreamlined *El Dorado,* two tracks over, will follow the *City* at a respectful distance (30 minutes). The antique observation car on the rear was for a special party. Photo by Richard Steinheimer, February 3, 1952.

Which *Daylight* from Los Angeles was better? The *Coast Daylight* ran along the edge of the Pacific for 113 miles, but the *San Joaquin Daylight* ran behind steam long after the *Coast Daylight* was dieselized, and its route terminated in the cavernous wood trainshed of Oakland Pier. Photo by Robert Hale.

The *Oakland Lark* gave East Bay residents fast overnight service to and from Los Angeles (the overnight *Owl* via the San Joaquin Valley had an older name but was considerably slower). Train 74 awaits its 8:30 p.m. departure on a foggy evening. Its consist includes a deadhead Pullman, a baggage car, a coach, and three streamlined Pullmans to turn over to the main section of the *Lark* at San Jose. Photo by Fred Matthews, January 27, 1952.

Pacific type 2484 stands on the tail track west of the trainshed after bringing train 255, the Oakland section of the *Coast Daylight,* from San Jose. Visible in the distance is a tower of the San Francisco-Oakland Bay Bridge. Photo by Richard Steinheimer.

Waiting for their next call at the West Oakland roundhouse are GS-2 4410, the first of the *Daylight* 4-8-4s, GS-3 4423, and GS-6 4469, the last 4-8-4 built for Southern Pacific. By the early 1950s they had been stripped of their streamlining and were used mostly in freight service but still handled San Joaquin Valley passenger trains. Photo by John C. Illman, May 24, 1953.

In 1954 Southern Pacific purchased a Budd Rail Diesel Car at the instigation of the California Public Utilities Commission. The railroad had petitioned to drop a pair of Oakland-Sacramento local trains, and the PUC suggested that SP try such cost-cutting measures as self-propelled diesel cars. Even with the new car and a faster schedule, patronage continued to decline, and SP finally was allowed to discontinue the trains in 1959 (it leased the car to Northwestern Pacific for service between Willits and Eureka). Car SP-10 pauses at 16th Street Station on the last day it held down the schedule of the steam-powered *Statesman.* The next day it received a flat 2-hour schedule for the 85-mile run, cutting 25 minutes off the old time. Visible are the upper level platforms that served the electric trains. Photo by John C. Illman, April 24, 1954.

One of SP's first group of 4-8-4s leads a fruit extra past 16th Street Station. An electric suburban train climbing the ramp to the upper level of the station is visible at the left edge of the photo. Photo by Earl Fancher, 1937, from the collection of Harre W. Demoro.

Cars 357 and 375, 1911 products of American Car & Foundry, stand at the west end of the San Francisco terminal. The 116-seat cars are posing as an inbound train; trains on these tracks in regular service would be heading away from the camera. Key System trains used the third rail. General Electric photo.

ELECTRIC LINES IN THE EAST BAY

The development of the East Bay cities of Oakland, Alameda, and Berkeley as bedroom communities for San Francisco was aided by Southern Pacific's local passenger service, which ran from Oakland Pier north to Berkeley and east through Oakland and from Alameda Pier through Alameda. Trains operated throughout the day and evening to connect with ferries to San Francisco. The frequency of the trains would be considered excellent urban transportation even today, and by 1911 train density had reached the point that SP electrified its suburban lines, some of which ran through city streets, with a 1200-volt DC catenary system. For most of their existence the electrified lines operated as the Oakland, Alameda & Berkeley Lines. On December 1, 1938, SP transferred the operation to a new subsidiary, the Interurban Electric Railway Company.

SP had a vigorous competitor in the East Bay, the Key System, a suburban trolley system that operated its own ferries to San Francisco. The Key System pier also served as the terminal for Sacramento Northern trains from Sacramento and Chico.

Patronage on SP's East Bay lines declined after the mid-1920s as passengers turned to automobiles for local trips, then for transbay trips as auto ferries began operation. As the Depression deepened, fewer and fewer people had jobs — and therefore fewer passengers rode the trains to work.

Commuting by automobile became easier and passenger counts on the trains plummeted when the San Francisco-Oakland Bay Bridge opened.

The bridge opened for highway traffic on November 12, 1936. On its upper deck were three lanes in each direction for automobiles, and on the lower deck were three lanes for buses and trucks and space for two tracks for the electric trains of the Key System, Sacramento Northern, and Southern Pacific. Tracklaying began in February 1938 and was complete by the end of the year, as was the six-track elevated terminal at First and Mission streets in San Francisco — known variously as the Eastbay Terminal, Bridge Terminal, Key System Terminal, Transbay Terminal, and Transbay Transit Terminal.

Rail passenger service began January 15, 1939. Electric trains ceased using Oakland Pier and most ferry schedules were discontinued then. When train service began across the Bay Bridge, SP's Oakland and Berkeley lines had 20-minute headways and the two Alameda lines each had 40-minutes headways. In December 1939 IER and Key System petitioned to reduce frequencies to cut expenses. SP's off-peak service was reduced on February 12, 1940, and two weeks later SP petitioned to cut all electric train service. On August 26, 1940, the Railroad Commission authorized abandonment; the ICC concurred on November 9, 1940. SP's Alameda and Oakland trains made their last runs early in the mornings of January 18 and 22, 1941, respectively; the last Berkeley trains ran on July 26, 1941.

The Key System expanded its operations onto SP's lines and continued to operate trains until April 20, 1958, when they became the victims of a state plan to rebuild Bay Bridge with five lanes on each deck — westbound on top and eastbound below.

Sacramento Northern's Sacramento trains ran only until August 26, 1940; commuter service between San Francisco and Pittsburg lasted until June 30, 1941.

Recommended reading: *Red Trains in the East Bay,* by Robert S. Ford, published in 1977 by Interurbans, P. O. Box 6444, Glendale, CA 91205 (ISBN: 0-916374-27-0).

Passengers from a train that has just arrived on track 2 stream down the ramp into the terminal while outbound passengers await their train on track 3. Photo by Fred Fellow, Jr., 1940.

Baggage motors 700 and 701 made several trips a day between Oakland Pier and downtown Berkeley carrying mail and express. In latter days the cars were bright red with black roof and underbody. Photo by Arthur R. Alter, December 1938.

At Adeline Street and Alcatraz Avenue in Berkeley SP's trains met Key System's Berkeley trains (at the right) and the local streetcars of East Bay Transit (a Key System affiliate). Photo by Fred Fellow, Jr.

North of downtown Berkeley SP's Shattuck Avenue trains ran through a pleasant residential neighborhood. Photo by Brian Thompson, 1941.

Trains terminated on Solano Avenue at Thousand Oaks. (The Oaks Theater was featuring *Tin Pan Alley,* starring Alice Faye.) A short tunnel (later used by Key System, now a road tunnel) led trains to the Northbrae area of Berkeley. Both photos, Fred Fellow, Jr.

The *San Joaquin Daylight,* train 52, swings around a curve near Pinole, barely into its run from Oakland Pier to Los Angeles. The power is No. 4420, a de-skirted, black-painted GS-3. Photo by David G. Edwards, May 1951.

Oakland to Sacramento

SP's principal main line out of Oakland ran north along the east shore of the bay through Emeryville and Berkeley, cut inland through Richmond, then followed the south shores of San Pablo Bay and Carquinez Strait to Martinez. There the line divided. The Mococo line, as it is called nowadays, continued east through Pittsburg and Antioch, then turned southeast to Tracy, where it met the route over Altamont Pass.

The route to Sacramento climbed out of Martinez to the Suisun Bay Bridge across the Carquinez Strait. From the north end of the bridge the eastbound track descended quickly to the level of the marshland along the bay (the westbound track had an easier grade). The line ran north-northeast through wetlands to Suisun-Fairfield, where it joined the original California Pacific line from Vallejo and Napa Junction. It continued northeast through agricultural country, where roads run square with the compass, passing through Elmira and Dixon. At Davis the passenger route to Oregon diverged northward and the Sacramento line curved eastward. From Davis to West Sacramento the line was on a series of trestles and fills crossing the Yolo Bypass, a low-lying area that is part of the flood-control system. At West Sacramento the line crossed Sacramento Northern's Woodland Branch at grade, then passed over the Sacramento River on a double-deck rail-highway drawbridge just before reaching the Sacramento station.

The line from Oakland to Martinez was built by the Northern Railway, chartered in 1871 and completed in 1878. Ferries connected Crockett, 6 miles west of Martinez, with the south end of the California Pacific Railroad at South Vallejo.

The California Pacific Rail Road was completed in 1870 between South Vallejo, where it connected with boats from San Francisco, and Sacramento. The line ran north from Vallejo a few miles, turned east to climb over a low pass in the hills to Suisun, then made as straight a line as possible for Sacramento (there was one curve a little east of Suisun and another at Davis).

Central Pacific's rail route through Oakland, Niles Canyon, Altamont Pass, and Stockton measured 140 miles (it was 125 by boat). The Northern Railway-California Pacific short cut was about 50 miles less and lacked the climb over Altamont Pass, 737 feet above sea level. Central Pacific's reaction to the upstart Northern Railway and California Pacific was to lease them in 1876. By 1879 the Northern had built a spur south from Suisun to the shore of Carquinez Strait at Benicia and placed in service a ferry that took entire trains across the strait to Port Costa, 4 miles west of Martinez.

The route along the shore also proved better for trains moving between Oakland and the San Joaquin Valley. Although the distance from Oakland to Tracy was 9 miles greater via Martinez, the route was almost gradeless.

Extra 5041 East is 10 minutes out of West Oakland yard, heading for Roseville. Diesels have recently displaced the three-cylinder 4-10-2 from the usual territory for the type, the Los Angeles and Rio Grande divisions. Photos by Fred Matthews, October 1951.

The *Statesman,* train 246, stops at Berkeley on a rainy morning shortly before it was replaced on the Oakland-Sacramento local run by a Budd Rail Diesel Car. Photo by Richard Steinheimer.

Six-wheel switcher 1241, built by Baldwin in 1918, switches a lumber yard near Ward Street and Shattuck Avenue in Berkeley, on the line formerly served by electric suburban trains. Photo by Don Matthews, April 1948.

Train 14, the *Beaver,* stops for passengers at the Berkeley station at the foot of University Avenue. The *Beaver* was an Oakland-Portland economy train, carrying coaches and tourist sleepers, plus a sleeper and a coach for Grants Pass. From Oakland to Portland it preceded the all-first-class *Cascade;* southward it followed by 20 minutes. The *Beaver* was replaced by the *Shasta Daylight* on July 9, 1949. Photo by Fred Matthews, September 1948.

The Chicago-bound *City of San Francisco* accelerates through Stege (a railroad point north of Berkeley) behind a trio of Alco diesels as train 27, the westbound *Overland,* with a *Daylight*-hued parlor-observation car on the rear, disappears toward Oakland Pier. Rare is the chance to photograph trains meeting on double track. Photo by John C. Illman, April 8, 1950.

Even on a holiday, SP is moving tonnage: 4-8-2s 4338 and 4365 lead Extra 4365 West past the station at Richmond. Photo by John C. Illman, November 11, 1949.

The *Gold Coast* from Chicago, train 23, makes an early-morning stop at Richmond. Engine 4415, one of the first group of *Daylight* 4-8-4s, has been stripped of its skirting and painted black. Photo by John C. Illman, March 30, 1952.

Train 55 rolls through El Sobrante, just east of Richmond, nearing the end of its 20 hour 45 minute trip from Los Angeles. Power for the train is a 4-8-2 with a skyline casing over the domes. Photo by David G. Edwards, 1949.

Light Pacific 2451 leads the second section of train 57, the *Owl* — tourist sleepers and a dining car, probably a troop movement — past the Pinole station. Photo by John C. Illman, July 10, 1949.

Passengers are finishing breakfast and gathering their luggage as train 101, the *City of San Francisco,* rolls along the shore of San Pablo Bay at Sobrante. Arrival at Oakland Pier is 30 minutes away. Photo by David G. Edwards.

A long string of heavyweight Pullmans brings up the rear of the overnight *Owl* from Los Angeles. Visible across San Pablo Bay are the hills of Marin County. Photo by David G. Edwards.

A 15-car *Shasta Daylight* curves along the bay at Pinole, 20 miles into its all-day-and-evening trip north to Portland. Photo by Fred Matthews, April 19, 1952.

Pacific 2488 leads train 229, the Sacramento-Oakland *Governor,* along the shore of San Pablo Bay at Pinole.
Photo by John C. Illman, August 11, 1951.

Mountain 4360 heads an extra freight eastward at the same point. Photo by John C. Illman, May 6, 1951.

Cab forward 4124, an AC-5 built by Baldwin in 1929, heads an eastbound freight at Crockett. The bridge visible in the distance carries U. S. Highway 40 across the Carquinez Strait. The mail car at the left edge of the picture was set out each day by train 56. Photo by John C. Illman, April 29, 1950.

Consolidations used in switching and local freight service congregate around the two-stall enginehouse at Port Costa. The track in the distance on which three cabooses are standing is the former lead to the ferry slip — until the completion of the Suisun Bay Bridge in 1930, trains were ferried across the Carquinez Strait. Photos by Fred Matthews, November 17, 1956.

GS-3 No. 4429, divested of its skirting and red-and-orange *Daylight* paint, leads an Oakland-bound freight along the waterfront between Martinez and Port Costa. Photo by Richard Steinheimer.

At the bottom of the photo a 4-8-2 waits in the middle siding at Ozol while a second freight passes on the west-bound main track and wraps itself around the curves. Photo by John C. Illman, September 23, 1950.

Passengers are aboard and the last hand baggage is being loaded into the baggage elevators. In a moment the *San Joaquin Daylight* will depart from Martinez for Fresno, Bakersfield, and Los Angeles. Photo by Frank Clodfelter.

While mail is being loaded onto train 57, the Los Angeles-Oakland *Owl,* Pacific 2481 drifts into Martinez with train 224, the Oakland-Sacramento *Senator.* Five minutes later, mail and passengers loaded, it picks its way over the switch that separates the lines to Tracy and to the Suisun Bay Bridge. Photos by Fred Matthews, April 22, 1950.

The rear car of the *Shasta Daylight,* train 10, is just passing the Martinez depot as the three Alco PAs begin their climb to the bridge. Moments later Mogul 1769, built by Baldwin in 1901 as a Vauclain compound, chuffs eastward on the Mococo line toward Tracy with a short freight. Photos by John C. Illman, September 23, 1950.

Against a background of industry Pacific 2473 lifts the Sacramento-bound late-afternoon *El Dorado* up to the Suisun Bay Bridge. The heavyweight, olive-green baggage-lounge car and coaches of train 248 are as traditional in appearance as the *Daylights* were radical. Photo by Richard Steinheimer.

THE SUISUN BAY BRIDGE

In 1929 and 1930 Southern Pacific built a bridge across the strait between Benicia and Martinez. The bridge is generally considered the longest (5,603 feet) and heaviest double-track railroad bridge west of the Mississippi River. The bridge replaced two huge four-track train ferries *Solano* and *Contra Costa* (named for the two counties they connected). The bridge was opened on October 15, 1930, and dedicated November 1, 1930, as the Martinez-Benicia Bridge (it is usually referred to as the Suisun Bay Bridge).

Cab-forward 4150, heading a Roseville-bound freight, has just moved onto the lift span of the bridge in this early-1950s view. The route from Oakland to Sacramento is the only double-track route out of the East Bay. Photo by Richard Steinheimer.

Cab-forward 4230 (Baldwin, 1942) leads a westbound freight across the bridge toward Martinez. The trailer on the flat car right behind the tender foretells things to come; the two stock cars immediately following will disappear from the railroad scene. Photo by Fred H. Matthews, September 1955.

The short, stiff grade from Martinez to the bridge required a helper engine on heavy trains. Consolidation No. 2644, built in 1902 as a Vauclain compound, is nearly done with its job assisting an eastbound freight up to the bridge. The 2-8-0 will cut off at Bahia, at the bottom of the east approach to the bridge, and return light to Port Costa for another assignment. Photo by John C. Illman, January 1, 1951.

Cab-forward 4111, an AC-5 built in 1929, leans into the curve at the Martinez end of the bridge on a deadhead move. Photo by David G. Edwards, 1952.

Train 101, the westbound *City of San Francisco,* rolls across the bridge behind three Alco passenger diesels — No. 6013 is leading. Early-morning mist obscures the hills on the Benicia side of the strait. Photo by John C. Illman, September 23, 1950.

Train 102, the *City of San Francisco,* is little more than an hour into its trip from Oakland to Chicago as it crosses the bridge from Martinez to Benicia. The numbering of the diesel units, E2A SF-1 and E6Bs SF-5 and SF-6, places the photo some time in late 1945 or early 1946. SP photo.

The *City of San Francisco* was advertised as "The fastest thing on wheels between San Francisco and Chicago" (39¾ hours at its best). It was an extra-fare train. The *Overland Limited* was once the best train on the route and had a much longer ancestry, but after the *City* began running daily in 1947 the *Overland* began to look as though its operators wanted to show just how many paint schemes they used on their passenger cars. Here 4419, still wearing its skirting but with its *Daylight* colors painted over in black, leads a consist of heavyweight and lightweight cars eastward near Sacramento. Photo by Donald Sims, December 30, 1949.

Pacific 2485 walks out of Sacramento with the six cars of train 243. Behind the baggage car are four of the suburban coaches usually found on Peninsula commute trains. At the left Mikado 3250 waits with a westbound freight on the track that bypasses the passenger station. Photo by J. C. Hammond.

Mikado 3313 and Southern Pacific-type 5000, the first of the class, lift a freight up the east slope of Altamont Pass. The Western Pacific line is behind the photographer; the highway is U. S. Route 50. Photo by W. E. Malloy, Jr., March 15, 1953.

OAKLAND TO SAN JOSE AND STOCKTON

Because water transportation was so easy, railroad development in the East Bay started later than it did in in the inland parts of the state, but by 1863 the San Francisco & Oakland Railroad was operating from a ferry wharf to East Oakland, and in 1865 the San Francisco & Alameda Railroad was open from a ferry terminal through Alameda and San Leandro to Hayward. The two railroads developed into the two Oakland-San Jose routes that Southern Pacific has even today.

The easterly route, built by the San Francisco & Oakland, followed First Street through Oakland, then ran straight to Niles. There it joined the Western Pacific (the first Western Pacific), which ran through Warm Springs and Milpitas (paralleling the latter-day Western Pacific, now Union Pacific) to San Jose.

The westerly route was built by the San Francisco & Alameda and the South Pacific Coast — and the South Pacific Coast is worth a brief digression. It was planned as a narrow gauge railroad to run from Alameda down the east shore of San Francisco Bay, then southwest across the Santa Clara Valley and the Coast Range to Santa Cruz. From there it would turn east, cross the Coast Range, the Sierra, and a whole bunch of desert, and eventually connect with the Denver & Rio Grande Western. It reached Santa Cruz in 1880, gave up its transcontinental ambitions, and was leased to Southern Pacific in 1887. SP standard-gauged the line in 1907. The part of the line from San Jose over the mountains to Santa Cruz was known for years as the route of the *Suntan Specials*, excursion trains from San Francisco to the beach at Santa Cruz. Storms washed out the line over the mountains in March 1940.

Much of the former South Pacific Coast route lay along the tideflats and marshes. It originally started at Alameda Pier, followed Encinal Avenue through Alameda, then crossed the mouth of San Leandro Bay to Bay Farm Island. That line is long since gone; a short connector leaves the other Oakland-San Jose route in San Leandro. The line made brief landfalls through Union City and Newark and joined the San Francisco-San Jose route at Santa Clara. During the 1940s and 1950s the Newark route was used by the *Oakland Lark* and the Oakland connection to the *Coast Daylight* because of the industry (and hence freight trains) along the Niles route.

The first rail route into the Bay Area from the east was the Western Pacific Rail Road (the first Western Pacific, not the George Gould-Feather River Canyon-*California Zephyr* Western Pacific of later years). It was a joint undertaking of the Central Pacific and the San Francisco & San Jose Railroad. Its line ran south from Sacramento through Stockton, west over Altamont Pass (737 feet above sea level) to present-day Pleasanton, then south through Niles Canyon and along the marshlands at the end of San Francisco Bay to San Jose. The intent was to bring Central Pacific trains into San Francisco by rail all the way. The roundabout route was necessary to avoid the delta of the Sacramento and San Joaquin rivers and the waters of San Francisco Bay. The line was completed from Sacramento to San Jose on September 15, 1869.

Nine days earlier, though, on September 6, the Western Pacific made a connection with the San Francisco & Alameda, creating a shorter, faster route to San Francisco, although it required a ferry ride at the end. Two months later, on November 8, 1869, the Western Pacific effected a connection with the San Francisco & Oakland, and Oakland became the principal terminal. By then the San Francisco & Alameda and the San Francisco & Oakland and their affiliated ferry lines were controlled by Central Pacific.

A decade later the route over Altamont Pass was superseded by the direct route southwest from Sacramento and along the shore of San Pablo Bay. The new route had the complication of the train ferry between Benicia and Port Costa, but it was 50 miles shorter and had no major grades. The Altamont Pass route remained useful for freight trains between the San Joaquin Valley and San Francisco, especially after the Dumbarton Bridge was completed in 1910, creating a route from Niles through Newark and across the bay to Redwood City.

Train 74, the *Oakland Lark,* runs along First Street as it departs Oakland's Jack London Square for San Jose. Its days are numbered; its last run was May 1, 1959, shortly after the photo was taken. Photo by Fred Matthews.

CAB-FORWARD ARTICULATED LOCOMOTIVES

In 1909 Baldwin delivered two 57-inch-drivered 2-8-8-2 Mallets, the first of that wheel arrangement, to replace double-headed Consolidations over the Sierra. They pulled well, but their length and exhaust were incompatible with the snowsheds — the crews couldn't see forward at all, and that problem was secondary to just breathing.

One trip made in reverse was more successful, except for difficulties with the tender, but it led to a suggestion: Put the cab over and around the smokebox. There were two major difficulties with that suggestion: The heat and noise would have been terrific, and the boiler overhang on curves left little room for a cab anyway. However, the proposal led to another solution to the problem: Separate the engine from the tender, attach the tender at the smokebox end, add plumbing to bring the fuel oil to the firebox, enclose the cab, and add headlight and pilot. The idea was outrageous, outlandish, and outstandingly successful.

Between 1909 and 1913 Baldwin shipped 47 of the type west. Between 1928 and 1931 most were rebuilt from Mallet compounds to simple articulateds and reclassified AC. They remained in service until the late 1940s.

SP tried the same concept for a passenger engine in 1911: a dozen MM-2-class cab-forward 2-6-6-2s. They proved unstable and by 1914 all had been fitted with four-wheel lead trucks. They were converted to simple locomotives in the late 1920s and 1930s and the entire class wound up in freight service in Oregon.

The second generation of cab-forwards consisted of 4-8-8-2s with 63-inch drivers and four 24-by-32-inch cylinders. The first ten arrived from Baldwin in 1928: Nos. 4100-4109, class AC-4. Baldwin kept on building cab-forwards until SP had 195 of the type in classes AC-4 through AC-12, except for AC-9. They were SP's trademark, even more than the *Daylight* 4-8-4s.

Although primarily mountain engines, the cab-forwards could be found on Southern Pacific's main lines in California, Oregon, and western Nevada (they sometimes worked east across Arizona and New Mexico, too), and they pulled heavy passenger trains as well as freights.

Recommended reading: *Cab-Forward*, by Robert J. Church, published in 1982 (revised edition) by Central Valley Railroad Publications, P. O. Box 116, Wilton, CA 95693

Cab-forward No. 4124 leads a freight south at East Oakland. Photo by Fred Matthews, June 27, 1950.

Type	Class	Numbers	Qty	Built	Retired	Notes
2-8-8-2	MC-1	4000, 4001	2	1909	1948, 1949	Rebuilt to AC-1
2-8-8-2	MC-2	4002-4016	15	1909	1935-1949	Rebuilt to AC-1
2-8-8-2	MC-4	4017-4028	12	1911	1935-1948	Rebuilt to AC-2
2-8-8-2	MC-6	4029-4048	20	1912-1913	1936-1949	Rebuilt to AC-3
4-6-6-2	MM-2	3900-3911	12	1911	1946-1948	Built as 2-6-6-2
4-8-8-2	AC-4	4100-4109	10	1928	1953-1955	
4-8-8-2	AC-5	4110-4125	16	1929	1952-1955	
4-8-8-2	AC-6	4126-4150	25	1930	1953-1955	
4-8-8-2	AC-7	4151-4176	26	1937	1954-1958	
4-8-8-2	AC-8	4177-4204	28	1939	1954-1958	
4-8-8-2	AC-10	4205-4244	40	1942	1955-1958	
4-8-8-2	AC-11	4245-4274	30	1942-1943	1954-1958	
4-8-8-2	AC-12	4275-4294	20	1943-1944	1955-1958	

The northbound *Oakland Lark* rolls north toward Oakland Pier. To the left is the Nimitz Freeway; at the right is Western Pacific's single-track line. Photo by Fred Matthews, June 27, 1950.

Pacific 2420, a P-4 rebuilt from an earlier P-1, brings the five cars of the *Daylight* connection north through Fruitvale under a series of signal bridges bearing arrays of lower-quadrant semaphore signals. Photo by William Edward White, 1948.

Train 255, the *Daylight* connection, clips through at Alviso, 8 miles north of San Jose, behind Pacific 2484, a P-10, largest and heaviest of SP's 4-6-2s. Photo by Richard Steinheimer.

Freights meet in Niles Canyon: The first section of train 406 approaches behind cab-forward 4117, while train 429 waits in the siding with 2-10-2 No. 3734. Baldwin built both locomotives, No. 4117 in 1929 and No. 3734 in 1924. Photo by Jack Wirick, 1952.

A train of empty gondolas rolls through Brightside in Niles Canyon on its way back to the gravel pit at Radum. Photo by David G. Edwards.

A Southern Pacific freight and Western Pacific's *Royal Gorge* work eastward through Altamont Pass shortly before the inauguration of the *California Zephyr* in 1949. Photo by Robert M. Hanft.

Train 401 climbs Altamont Pass behind cab-forward 4102, heading toward Redwood Junction and San Francisco.
Photo by John C. Illman, September 9, 1952.

Train 51, the *San Joaquin Daylight* from Los Angeles, and train 53, the *Sacramento Daylight,* stand side by side at Lathrop. The Los Angeles-Sacramento cars of No. 51 will be switched here to 53, which originated at Tracy.
Photo by Donald K. Hedgpeth.

A 2-8-4 purchased secondhand from the Boston & Maine leads a freight southward at French Camp tower, the crossing of the Tidewater Southern just south of Stockton. The Lima-built 2-8-4s were not B&M's handsomest locomotives, and removing the Coffin feedwater heater, painting the smokebox front silver, and substituting a whaleback tender has not helped matters. Photo by Fred Matthews, August 5, 1950.

The smallest of the *Daylight* engines was Atlantic 3000, shown getting the *Sacramento Daylight* rolling at Stockton. At Lathrop the two pairs of articulated coaches on the rear will be switched onto train 52 from Oakland. The locomotive was built in 1907 as 3058, and rebuilt in 1927 as second 3000. Photo by Fred Matthews, October 25, 1947.

Six-wheel switcher 1252 shuffles stock cars at, appropriately, Stockton. Photo by Waldemar Sievers, 1939; collection of Harre W. Demoro.

Northwestern Pacific train 2 is 20 minutes into its 10-hour trip from San Rafael to Eureka as it passes through then-rural Novato. The hood over the headlight was a World War II modification. Trains 1 and 2 were discontinued in May 1942. Photo by Arthur Lloyd.

Northwestern Pacific

Across the Golden Gate from San Francisco is Marin County: mountains, seacoast, sheltered valleys, redwoods, equable climate. In the early years of this century it would have been hard to find a more idyllic place to live.

By the end of the 1870s the San Francisco & North Pacific reached from Tiburon, on San Francisco Bay, north through Petaluma and Santa Rosa. It was leased to a new company, the California Northwestern, in 1898. The narrow gauge North Pacific Coast Railroad was completed from Sausalito north through San Anselmo to Tomales on the coast, then back inland to the Russian River. In 1902 the North Pacific Coast came under new management and was renamed the North Shore Railroad. In response to growing traffic, it standard-gauged, double-tracked, and electrified its lines south of San Rafael and Mill Valley.

In 1903 the Southern Pacific acquired the California Northwestern and the North Shore and talked of extending lines north to Eureka, into territory where the Santa Fe owned two isolated railroads. SP and Santa Fe quickly recognized that the territory could never support two railroads and jointly formed the Northwestern Pacific Railroad, which was completed through to Eureka in 1914.

NWP's electric service from the ferry terminal at Sausalito to San Rafael, the county seat, helped Marin County develop into a suburban area — but not very fast. The population of the country was 15,702 in 1900, 27,342 in 1920, and 41,648 in 1930, mostly in the 10-mile distance between Sausalito and San Rafael. Spurred by commuter groups, in the 1920s NWP upgraded and modernized the commuter service. The most conspicuous part of the program was a group of 19 steel cars. In 1929 SP purchased Santa Fe's share of the NWP, and between 1930 and 1933 NWP abandoned its narrow gauge lines beyond the suburban area of Marin County.

In 1923 the state legislature formed a bridge district, moving the proposals for a bridge across the entrance to San Francisco Bay nearer to fruition. The first phase of engineering work was completed and voters approved a bond issue in 1930. The Golden Gate Bridge was completed May 27, 1937. Commuters immediately began using their own automobiles or Greyhound buses from Marin County to downtown San Francisco. The vehicles were more modern than NWP's coaches and ferries and service was direct — there was no need to change from train to ferry at Sausalito. NWP's owner Southern Pacific wasn't especially worried about loss of business; SP owned a sizable chunk of Pacific Greyhound. NWP briefly tried to compete but gave up. The last commuter trains and ferries ran on February 28, 1941. (In 1990 Marin County's population was 230,000, and its main north-south highway, U. S. 101, is packed solid much of each day.)

After March 1, 1941, NWP had just two passenger trains in its timetables, daytime and overnight trains covering the 278 miles between Sausalito and Eureka. On November 23, 1941, the company shifted the southern terminus of the trains from Sausalito to San Rafael, and discontinued the day train in May 1942. The night train continued until June 2, 1956, when it was replaced by the triweekly, daytime *Redwood*. On November 9, 1958, the *Redwood* became a Willits-Eureka train, with Greyhound buses covering the San Francisco-San Rafael-Willits run. A Budd Rail Diesel Car replaced the specially lettered coaches of the *Redwood* in 1959; the train continued to operate until April 30, 1971.

Recommended reading: *Electric Railway Pioneer*, by Harre W. Demoro, published in 1983 by Interurban Press, P. O. Box 6444, Glendale, CA 91205 (ISBN 0-916374-55-6)

Passengers board an electric train to San Rafael at Sausalito. The passengers' coats say "winter," and notices posted on the columns may well be warnings of the final discontinuance of service. SP photo.

A single car rolls past Tamalpais High School on the Mill Valley Branch. Photo by W. C. Whittaker, 1937.

A train from San Rafael enters the station at San Anselmo heading for Sausalito. The line diverging to the left goes to Fairfax. Photo by B. H. Ward.

Northwestern Pacific had only two connections with the rest of the country's railroad network: a junction with Southern Pacific at Schellville, south of Sonoma, and a ferry slip at Tiburon that served as the interchange point with Santa Fe. Three old flatcars used as idlers keep the weight of General Electric 44-tonner No. 1902 off the apron as it loads the car float. Photo by Robert Hale, 1956.

After the southern terminal of the Eureka trains shifted from Sausalito to San Rafael, the trains were turned and serviced at Tiburon and dead-headed to San Rafael to receive passengers. Train 4, the overnight to Eureka, hustles across Reed Trestle, just out of Tiburon. At San Rafael it will pick up mail and express cars, then depart at 6:30 for redwood country. The train will be considerably longer leaving San Rafael, and the road engine, Ten-Wheeler 2320, will require the assistance of Pacific 2459 up a short but stiff grade out of San Rafael. Photo by Don Howe.

A train of outbound freight — primarily lumber — follows Southern Pacific 2-8-0 No. 2561 around the north shore of San Pablo Bay, heading for the SP interchange at Schellville. Photo by Jim Morley.

A freight moving from the SP at Schellville to the NWP main line at Ignacio rolls across the mouth of the Petaluma River at Black Point. Photo by A. C. Kalmbach, April 1950.

Train 1, the day train from Eureka, awaits departure time at Santa Rosa. Photo by Arthur Lloyd.

RECESS FOR RAILROADING

"Lookit, Charlotte, here it comes. I'm not scared — are you? This one's not streamliney like those others I've seen. You know what, Charlotte? My daddy showed me one of those black ones with the great big wheels when we went to visit Grandma and Grandpa Holt in Oakland last summer. It was inside a building. My daddy says the engineers used those black ones when I was a little girl. My daddy says he wishes his teacher had taken him for a ride on a train when he was in school. Can you see the engineer, Charlotte? That silver car — that's the one we ride in. Isn't it funny how that train can stay on those little rails — without anything to hold onto, I mean. And even around curves and up and down hills. A railroad is a very great thing, I think. Stand here in front of me, Char, so we can be partners. I'm not scared — are you?"

— *Rosemary Entringer* (from *Trains* Magazine, July 1957).

Rosemary Entringer joined Trains *Magazine in 1948 and was its managing editor from early 1954 until her death in July 1977. Her insistence on spelling, grammar, and literacy was evident in each issue of the magazine; her own writing appeared but rarely.*

Train 4, the *Redwood,* makes a flag stop at Novato to receive a group of children who will ride 10 miles north to Petaluma — for most of them, their first train ride. Photo by Richard Steinheimer, January 1957.

The longest and heaviest double-track railroad bridge west of the Mississippi River is still doing the job it was built for, but no longer in isolation. Interstate Highway 680 now arches high above Carquinez Strait just west of Southern Pacific's bridge. Scarlet-and-orange Alco PAs and two-tone gray or Armour yellow passenger cars have yielded to the red, white, and blue of Amtrak: F40s 305 and 240 lead train 11, the Seattle-Los Angeles *Coast Starlight* into Martinez. Photo by Hugh B. Harvey, July 9, 1987.

Like the PAs, SP's Fairbanks-Morse Train Masters have been replaced by F40s. Moreover, "Southern Pacific" has been replaced by "CalTrain," and, though it is not immediately obvious from the photo, push-pull operation is the norm in Peninsula commute service. Photo by George H. Drury, February 27, 1989.

SOUTHERN PACIFIC TODAY

Peninsula Commute Service

Third Street Station in San Francisco was torn down in 1976 and replaced with a small station a block west at Fourth and Townsend streets. On July 1, 1980, the California Department of Transportation (CalTrans) signed an agreement with Southern Pacific to finance the Peninsula commute service. Trains were added to the timetable in 1981, and 1985 saw the delivery of the first of 20 F40PH-2 diesels by Electro-Motive and 73 gallery coaches by Nippon Sharyo.

In 1991 San Francisco, San Mateo, and Santa Clara counties purchased the San Francisco-San Jose line. Responsibility for the service was shifted to the Peninsula Corridor Joint Powers Board, retaining the CalTrain name for the service. The agency has extended the service to Gilroy, about 30 miles beyond San Jose.

East Bay

Except for the short piece of track from the West Oakland wye to Oakland Pier and the former (old) Western Pacific route over Altamont Pass, the main lines are all still in place and all busy. Almost nothing remains of the electrified lines in Oakland, Alameda, and Berkeley.

Marin County

Little trace remains of Northwestern Pacific's lines in southern Marin County. The knowing eye can still find bits of roadbed and see the pattern of the tracks repeated in the streets at the center of San Anselmo. North and east of Ignacio the line is still in use, owned by the new Northwestern Pacific Railroad Authority.

Amtrak

In early 1971 SP had four long-distance trains serving San Francisco and Oakland: the *Coast Daylight* (San Francisco-Los Angeles), the *San Joaquin Daylight* (Oakland-Los Angeles), the *Cascade* (Oakland-Portland), and the *City of San Francisco* (Oakland-Ogden, with through cars to Chicago and Kansas City). Amtrak's *Coast Starlight* combines the *Coast Daylight* (rerouted to Oakland) and the *Cascade;* the *California Zephyr* duplicates the *City* as far east as Wells, Nevada. Amtrak restored train service to the San Joaquin Valley in 1974; the four daily *San Joaquins* use SP rails as far as Port Chicago, east of Martinez. Amtrak's *Capitols*, inaugurated in 1991, recreate the

Senator, Statesman, and *El Dorado,* and reach beyond Oakland to San Jose and beyond Sacramento to Roseville.

Amtrak came to find 16th Street Station less than satisfactory as a terminal. Its location in a rugged neighborhood nowhere near downtown Oakland was a liability, and it could handle only one train at a time. The earthquake of 1989 helped decide matters — it severely damaged the building. In 1993 Amtrak began using a new station at Emeryville, just north of the east end of the Bay Bridge approach, for passengers transferring to buses to San Francisco, and in 1994 moved its Oakland stop to a new station (and the location of a station long ago) in Jack London Square. In San Francisco Amtrak's buses stop at the Ferry Building at the foot of Market Street.

AUTHOR'S CONFESSION

I wasn't born a Southern Pacific enthusiast; I was made one. I grew up measuring all railroads against the Boston & Maine. SP and B&M didn't have much in common, except maybe more 2-6-0s than up-to-date railroads should have. However, three decades ago I lived in San Francisco for six years. I came to know the city's ancient and venerable institutions, one of which was the Southern Pacific Company. My relationship with SP developed on several levels. At the outset it was employer-employe (they spelled employe with only one e at the end), and it took SP about a year to reach the conclusion that I wasn't meant to be a computer programmer (SP was quicker at it than I).

I was also an occasional passenger, both local and long-distance. Visiting friends down the Peninsula was easier by train than by car, particularly at the end of the evening. Most of my travel during those years was by train, and SP had more trains that went more places than the other roads. I developed into a critic, I'm sorry to say, and sometimes an apologist, usually in response to "I rode one of your trains once."

And I became an SP enthusiast. The late 1960s and early 1970s were not golden years for railroading in the Bay Area but neither were they lead or zinc. Two long-distance trains, the *Coast Daylight* and the *Lark,* and one medium-distance train, the *Del Monte,* added variety to the Fairbanks-Morse Train Masters and gallery cars of the Peninsula commute fleet. The East Bay had four daily passenger trains — the *San Joaquin Daylight, Cascade, City of San Francisco,* and nameless, nocturnal 21 and 22, the Overland Route mail train — and freight trains were plentiful. Even if SP's gray diesels weren't as attractive as the warbonnet-painted F units on Santa Fe's *San Francisco Chief* and SP's trains lacked the uniformity of WP's *California Zephyr,* there were more of them. When I went out to take pictures, I knew I'd be far more likely to encounter a train on SP than on WP or Santa Fe.

Friends showed me not only the active places of railroading in the Bay Area but also the historic places: places like Baltimore Park substation on the Northwestern Pacific and SP's former main line through San Francisco's Mission District. One day we drove out to the site of Oakland Pier. There was nothing there any more. I didn't know then what Oakland Pier had been.

I'm not one to weep over things I never did or saw, but as I selected the photos for this book I wished I could have seen Oakland Pier. For now I can see Oakland Pier only through the photographs of Bob Hale, John Illman, Fred Matthews, and Dick Steinheimer, but if I don't find Oakland Pier in the next life (full of *Daylight*-colored 4-8-4s and PAs), the Presbyterian Church will have to do some fast explaining. — *GHD*

INDEX OF PHOTOGRAPHS

ABOUT THE PHOTOGRAPHERS

Three photographers are responsible for most of the photos in this book:

John C. Illman was born in 1921 and grew up in Seattle and Vancouver, near the trains of the Great Northern and the cars of the British Columbia Electric Railway. He attended the University of Washington and met his future wife, Marjorie Kincaid, while they were both at the university's Friday Harbor Oceanographic Laboratory. They settled in the East Bay where John spent most of his working years as a research chemist for Shell Oil.

About 1948 on a whim he tried out Marjorie's new camera on the trains on Santa Fe's Oakland line that ran across the street from the house. Soon afterward, he rode a Southern Pacific *Suntan Special* to Santa Cruz. He was hooked. He kept on taking pictures of trains, and he joined the California-Nevada Railroad Historical Society. His first photo submission to *Trains* Magazine was a photo of a public relations special that followed the inaugural run of the *California Zephyr*. It was accepted and rated a full page in the October 1949 issue of the magazine. His work has also appeared in *Railroad, Railfan & Railroad, Pacific Rail News, Passenger Train Journal*, and *Vintage Rails*. He and Marjorie live on an island in Puget Sound when they aren't traveling.

Fred Matthews is a native of San Francisco. In the mid-1940s he frequently visited relatives who owned a Gravenstein apple orchard northwest of Sebastopol. Through the orchard ran the decrepit track and catenary of the Petaluma & Santa Rosa Railroad, long-since freight-only. Often in midafternoon the wires would begin to hiss, then a loud humming and buzzing would signal the passage of ancient freight motor, its mellow pneuphonic horn sounding for a nearby crossing. To a ten-year-old this was an overwhelming experience — like encountering a dragon. In early 1946 the dragons vanished, replaced by bright 44-ton diesels, then reappeared, stored in Sebastopol. Fred badgered his family into dusting off a folding Kodak as old as the freight motors, and he snapped some photos of the dragons.

There followed an endless search for better cameras and more dramatic pictorial records of the scene. Being a railfan in the decade after 1945 influenced Fred's choice of career: historians know that Things Change. He carried his camera along to graduate school in Boston, then to England for two years, just in time to see steam vanish, then to Toronto for a quarter century of teaching. He continues to photograph and write about railroads half a century since the dragons of Sebastopol. His work has appeared in all the major railroad magazines and in his two-volume book, *Northern California Railroads: The Silver Age*.

Richard Steinheimer's first published railroad photo was of a Pacific Electric car that split a switch at North Glendale and was occupying a double-track line all by itself. He became a photographer for the Glendale *News-Press*. One summer day while doing man-in-the-street interviews about the smog ("No, it's okay here, but I notice it a lot in L.A.") he realized his eyes were watering and his throat was burning. Dick moved north to San Rafael to take a job with the *Independent-Journal* as a photographer and eventually as editor of the weekly magazine section. He later turned to industrial photography. His photography has been featured in *Trains* Magazine for decades, and he has several books to his credit: *Backwoods Railroads of the West, Western Trains* (with Donald Sims), the two volumes of *Growing Up With Trains* (one co-authored by Donald Sims, the other by Ted Benson), and *The Electric Way Across the Mountains*, published in 1980 by Carbarn Press. Dick and his wife, Shirley Burman, are industrial photographers in Sacramento.